Walks from your car

North-East Derbyshire

by
Astrid & Ray Russell

Dalesman Books
1985

The Dalesman Publishing Company Ltd.,
Clapham, via Lancaster, LA2 8EB
First published 1985

© Astrid & Ray Russell 1985

ISBN: 0 85206 825 5

Printed by: Swannack, Brown & Co. Ltd., Hull, England.

Contents

Cover map by Barbara Yates
Maps in the text by the authors
Drawings by Alison and Helena Russell

An Introduction

BORDERING on the eastern edge of the Peak National Park is the area of North East Derbyshire. Whilst the region is industrial in parts it also boasts large rural areas of great beauty and rich evidence of man's activity in preceding centuries. The hills, dales and moorland of the area are close to large urban centres and yet, probably because of its proximity to the Peak Park, the region is much less visited than it deserves to be. Consequently some of its many rights of way are under-used and in parts are beginning to show some signs of neglect, though not enough to make walking difficult and spoil the enjoyment. We hope that this book will assist and encourage exploration of this fascinating area and that with increased usage its footpaths and stiles will become more known, more cared for and better preserved for enjoyment by future generations.

All of the routes described are circular and most include some footpath walking, some rough lane walking and the occasional stretch of walking on quiet roads. Most walks, especially in the winter months, have the occasional wet and muddy patch so walking boots or wellies are essential footwear. On many of the walks you will come across a site of particular historical significance. Whether it is an old industrial chimney or an ancient 'cruck' barn do pause long enough to reflect, for the sites form an integral part of the local heritage.

All the paths have been recently walked and should therefore be followed without difficulty. However if you come across an obstruction to the right of way you are following do bring it to the attention of the local council which has the right by law to take responsibility for clearing the obstruction if, as occasionally happens, the landowner cannot be persuaded to do it.

We are sure you will enjoy discovering this varied and interesting area.

Maps

It is intended that all the walks can be followed by even the most novice walker from the description given. However, use of the appropriate Ordnance Survey map will provide additional help and information. Maps useful with this book are:

Ordnance Survey Sheet 119 (Buxton, Matlock and Dove Dale).
Ordnance Survey Sheet 120(Mansfield and the Dukeries).
Ordnance Survey Map 'The White Peak' (East Sheet).

On any walk please observe the Country Code.

Ashover - Cocking Tor - Ashover

A not too strenuous climb leads to a glorious viewpoint above the Amber valley and the route then descends through a former lead-mining site before returning to Ashover by way of an ancient pack-horse road.

Distance: 2¾ miles (4.5 km)
Parking: In the public car park by the village hall at Ashover.
Time: About 2 hours.

FROM the village hall turn left down the main street past the church and turn right at the Red Lion. Walk along the road to where the wall on the left ends and a rough lane leads down to the river. As you descend this lane look up to the top of the hillside on the opposite side of the valley and see the line of stone slabs forming a fence along the skyline. This type of field boundary is a notable feature of the landscape around Ashover, due to the availability of stone from the many quarries in the area. Cross the river Amber and immediately over the bridge notice across the field on the left the levelled course of the former Ashover Light Railway. The bridge which carried it over the river has gone but its position is obvious. This railway was opened in 1925 principally for transporting minerals to the works of the Clay Cross Co., though it also ran a limited passenger service. It was operational for only 25 years.

Go straight ahead passing on your right the ruins of Ashover Corn Mill which fell into disuse in the late 19th century. Climb the opposite hillside keeping close to the left of the scrub. Shortly before the fence at the top an obvious path running along the contour is reached. Turn right along it and after a short distance find a steep narrow path on the left which climbs behind a large tree to a stile in the slab fence. Cross the field keeping the wall on your right to reach a stile beside the gateway ahead which leads into a hedged track. Go straight forward along the track to emerge into a minor road.

Turn right for a short distance and on reaching a house go over a stone stile beside a gate on your left. Keep to the right of an old barn and the path follows the wall on the right uphill and soon becomes an obvious holloway along which the passage of foot and horse traffic over several centuries has 'hollowed out' the level of the track. On reaching the wood above climb the stile and keep to the track through the trees until it emerges onto the road at Holestone.

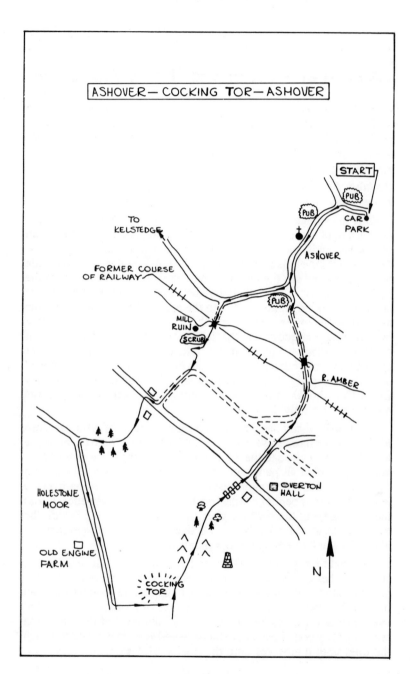

ASHOVER—COCKING TOR—ASHOVER

START

PUB

PUB

CAR PARK

TO KELSTEDGE

ASHOVER

FORMER COURSE OF RAILWAY

PUB

MILL RUIN

SCRUB

R. AMBER

HOLESTONE MOOR

OVERTON HALL

OLD ENGINE FARM

COCKING TOR

N

Turn left and walk along the road to reach Old Engine Farm on the right. This curious name refers to the siting here in the 18th century of a large steam engine to pump water from some of the many lead mines in the area. Ignore the footpath opposite the farm and continue on the road to take the next signposted footpath on the left. Go straight across the field to the old quarry at Cocking Tor. Walk through the quarry to the Tor beyond from where there are magnificent views over the Amber valley and far beyond. Hardwick Hall and Bolsover Castle are clearly visible on a good day. Take one of the steep but well-worn paths descending to the bridleway which runs below.

On reaching the bridleway turn left along it. Follow the track downhill and across the spoil heaps of former lead workings, passing a distinctive chimney below. At the end of the wood the track becomes paved and is intermittently so for the rest of its course back to Ashover. The paving dates from times when pack-horses carried salt and other goods along this ancient way. When a cross-roads is reached go straight on to the next where the driveway from Overton Hall bears right downhill.

Climb the stile through the slab fence to the left of the gateposts and continue down the field. Stone steps at the bottom of the field take you through a stile and soon bring you into an old lane. Follow the lane down to the river and then on back up to the village.

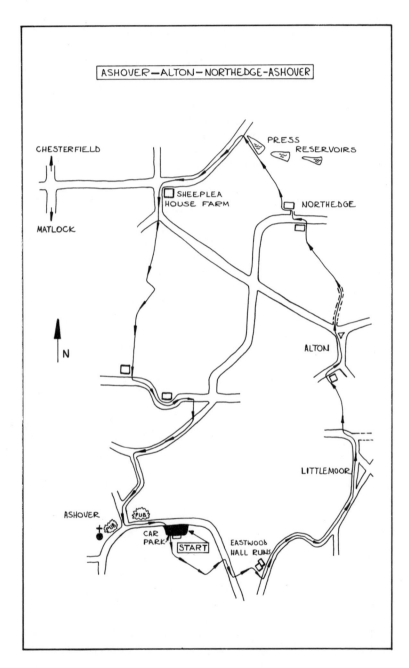

ASHOVER — ALTON — NORTHEDGE — ASHOVER

PRESS RESERVOIRS

CHESTERFIELD

SHEEPLEA HOUSE FARM

NORTHEDGE

MATLOCK

N

ALTON

LITTLEMOOR

ASHOVER

PUB
PUB

CAR PARK

START

EASTWOOD HALL RUINS

10

Ashover - Alton - Northedge - Ashover

A walk giving superb views in many directions. After climbing steadily the route becomes fairly level and footpaths and quiet roads lead through several upland hamlets before a panoramic descent back to Ashover.

Distance: 4½ miles (just over 7 km).
Parking: In the public car park by the village hall at Ashover.
Time: Almost 2½ hours.

CROSS the recreation ground behind the car park and pass the children's swings to reach a stile in the wall at the end of the hedge on the right. Turn left through the stile into a green lane. At the second gate, where the lane ends and becomes a path, go through the gate and turn sharp left towards a stile at the bottom of the field. Continue through the next field and into Hardmeadow Lane. Turn right and walk along the road until, just before a farm, a stile beside a gate on the left is reached. Go through the stile and follow the path across the fields, with a wall and then a hedge on the right, towards Eastwood Hall. Turn right through a stile immediately before the house and emerge into a minor road. The ivy-clad ruin is all that remains of the 'New Hall' built in the early 17th century to replace the existing farmhouse of the Reresby family. After the Civil War parliament ordered many castles and large houses to be demolished to prevent them falling into Royalist hands again. Despite the owner at that time having eventually sided with the Roundheads, Eastwood Hall was firstly shot at with cannon from the hill behind, then attacked with picks and crowbars and finally blown up with gunpowder!

Turn left and continue until the road joins another at Littlemoor. Go forward through the village and take the road on the left named Alton Lane. This stretch of road gives glorious views towards Clay Cross, Stretton and Ogston Reservoir. Some distance along the road and shortly after passing a road junction on the right the road bends sharply to the left. Go through the stile in the wall on the right immediately after the bend. Go straight across the field aiming for a wall which curves in from the right. Keeping this wall close on your right continue straight ahead through a stile and then a gate into a lane along the left-hand side of a house and shortly into the road at Alton. Turn right down the road and take the next road on the left. Keep left where the road forks and cross the next road to continue up the rough lane almost opposite. The lane bears right between two houses then continues, bearing slightly left and becoming an obvious path, through gates and stiles over fields. On a clear day many church spires feature in the extensive view from this part of the walk. In the third field, when the buildings at Northedge can be seen over the wall at the bottom left-hand corner, watch for a stile in the wall on the left. Go through the stile and turn right to follow the wall down the field and eventually through a gate beside a house and into the road at Northedge.

Turn left up the road and soon turn right at a footpath sign into a farm road. Follow the road to the left immediately before a large house and the path turns to the right around the end of the farm buildings, through two gateways and continues straight ahead into fields. The path is clear now leading through fields and stiles towards Press Reservoirs. Walk alongside the top reservoir and keeping the reservoir boundary wall on your right eventually cross a stile into Birkin Lane. Follow the road left uphill to the crossroads at the top and take the left turn beside Sheeplea House Farm.

A fork in the road is soon reached and a footpath sign at this road junction indicates a way over the fields. The path continues almost in a straight line but is very difficult to follow in places as it is rarely walked and crop cultivation often obscures the route. However, do persevere as the eventual view over Ashover fully compensates for any difficulty encountered.

Cross the first field almost diagonally to find a stile a little to the right of a short stretch of wall about halfway along the opposite boundary. Keeping in the same direction cross the corner of the next field to find a step stile in the righthand wall. Bear left towards the bottom far corner of the field to find a stile just above the wall corner. Now continue forward over the next field to a step stile some distance along the wall on your right. Cross the next field making for the start of the wall opposite and keep the wall on your left until a gate is reached. Through the gate bear right to cross a large field diagonally towards two large trees on the opposite slope. The stile is rather obscured by bushes in the bottom corner of the field. Now make for a gateway straight ahead and go through a stile alongside it. Keep to the wall on the left and climb over it when a step stile is reached. Bear right down the field side and over a stile onto the road. Here a delightful view of Ashover and the Amber valley is suddenly revealed.

Turn left and walk along the road until, having passed Apple Tree Knoll House, you find a stile on either side of the road shortly before a crossroads. Go through the stile on the right and a paved path leads between the gorse bushes to the road below. Turn right down the hill, then left at the road junction. This part of Ashover has the curious name of Rattle. Many stocking-makers lived in the houses around here and the noise of their machines gave the area its name. Follow the road back into Ashover passing on the left a training department of the E.M.E.B. This building was one of two centres for hydropathic treatments which were established in Ashover in the mid-19th century. However, they were over-shadowed by the larger establishments at Matlock and had ceased to function as hydros by about 1900.

Ashover has many interesting features and a fine old church worthy of further exploration if you have the time.

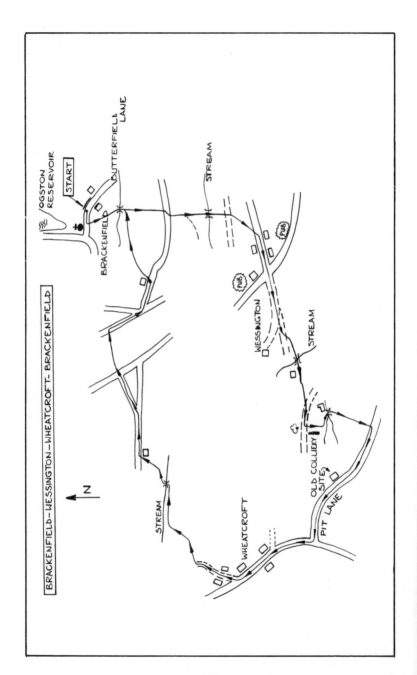

BRACKENFIELD–WESSINGTON–WHEATCROFT–BRACKENFIELD

N

OGSTON RESERVOIR

START

BRACKENFIELD

BUTTERFIELD LANE

STREAM

Pub

pub

WESSINGTON

STREAM

OLD COLLIERY SITE

PIT LANE

WHEATCROFT

STREAM

14

Brackenfield - Wessington - Wheatcroft - Brackenfield

Field footpaths and quiet roads lead through unspoilt mid-Derbyshire farmland.

Distance: Almost 5 miles (7.5 km).
Parking: On the roadside near Brackenfield church.
        Map reference 373590.
Time: About 2¾ hours.

GO through a stile a little way down Butterfield Lane and opposite the church. Bear slightly left across the field and cross a ditch by means of a slab bridge and then continue ahead, with the hedge on the left, through two more stiles. At the far side of the next field go through another stile and then go forward with the hedge and a ditch now on the right. The next stile leads into a road. Across the road and a little to the right is a signposted footpath. Following the direction of the sign cross two fields, ignoring a clear path to the right at the beginning of the second. Cross a stile and clapper bridge over a stream somewhat hidden in the bushes. The minerals in the ground around here give this small stream a distinctive orange colour on occasions. Climb the field at the other side of the bridge, keeping to the hedge on the right, and cross a stile into a rough track. Go through the stile opposite and bearing slightly right cross the field to another stile in the wall by a gate which brings you into the road at Wessington.

Turn right and walk along the road through the village and cross the main Matlock road to continue along a lane immediately opposite. After some distance a driveway goes off to a house on the right and the lane continues as a rough track. A little way down the track go through a stile beside a gate on the left. Cross the field diagonally and go through a stile just below a gate. Turn right and follow the hedge to a stream and wooden bridge. In autumn an abundance of crab apples, hazelnuts and other fruits can often be found on this stretch of the walk. Beyond the bushes at the other side of the bridge take the right-hand path down a bank, through trees and eventually emerge into a field on the left. Keeping near to the hedge on the right continue to reach a farm lane.

Walk to a large tree a little way to the right along the lane then turn left and walk up the field roughly parallel to the hedge on the right.

About halfway along the hedge at the top is a stile leading to a slab bridge and another stile. Go straight across the next field to a stream at the far side then turn left and follow the stream to an unusual stile made of hawthorn stumps. Keep the stream on your right until on approaching a house turn right through a squeezer stile, across a brook and over a wooden stile. Keeping the hedge on the left walk across the fields to the road.

This road is called Pit Lane and gets its name from the former Moorwood Moor colliery which closed over 100 years ago. Now turn right to pass the site of the colliery as you continue up the hill to turn right again at the road junction. Go through the hamlet of Wheatcroft and a little way beyond Wheatcroft House a track turns off right, leading through a farmyard and continuing beyond the gate at the other side. Where the track ends climb the stile and then go diagonally down the field to an old stone stile in the bottom left-hand corner. Cross the next field to the hedge opposite and follow it downhill to find a stile on the left towards the bottom of the field, concealed by holly bushes. The stile leads over a slab bridge and through a squeezer stile. Now turn right to the next squeezer stile and then bear left diagonally across the field to climb a stile beside a house and emerge into a lane.

Turn right along the lane, keeping left where the road forks and continue to reach the main road. The bridleway almost opposite leads between hedges to the road at Brackenfield Green where you should turn right and then take the second road on the left called Millers Lane. Take the signposted path on the left just beyond a cottage. Climb the wooden stile into a field then bear right to a squeezer stile among the bushes and go straight ahead to another. Go forward to the hedge at the bottom of the field and turn left to retrace your steps back to Brackenfield church.

The church is Victorian and not of particular interest but is worth a brief visit as it contains a rood-screen taken from a local and now ruined chapel, built between 1520-30, which the present church replaced. From the churchyard there is an attractive view of Ogston Reservoir.

AN UNUSUAL STILE NEAR WESSINGTON.

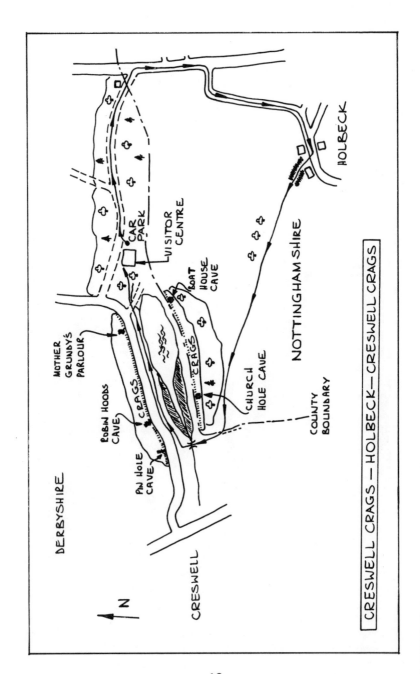

CRESWELL CRAGS — HOLBECK — CRESWELL CRAGS

N

DERBYSHIRE

CRESWELL

MOTHER GRUNDY'S PARLOUR

ROBIN HOODS CAVE

PIN HOLE CAVE

CRAGS

CRAGS

BOAT HOUSE CAVE

CHURCH HOLE CAVE

CAR PARK

VISITOR CENTRE

NOTTINGHAMSHIRE

COUNTY BOUNDARY

HOLBECK

18

Creswell Crags - Holbeck - Creswell Crags

A short walk on the borders of North East Derbyshire and Nottinghamshire passing through an impressive limestone gorge.

Distance: Just over 2 miles (4 km).
Parking: The car park at Creswell Crags Visitors' Centre.
        Map reference 538744.
Time: Including time to explore, about 2 hours.

NO books of walks on North East Derbyshire would be complete without a walk on the Derbyshire coal measures. This is it! But although this walk provides occasional spectacular views of nearby mining operations its main feature is the limestone gorge of Creswell Crags. This internationally important gorge contains several caves which have yielded rich evidence of occupation by both man and animals in prehistoric times. The Visitors' Centre provides an interesting presentation of what life must have been like for the inhabitants of the caves.

From the carpark continue down the tree-lined driveway until you reach the main road. Turn right into the road and after a short distance turn right again into the quiet minor road signposted Holbeck. Follow the road into the pleasant Nottinghamshire village of Holbeck and opposite a telephone box find a path on the right signposted Creswell Crags. The path goes between hedges then leads over a stile and into the fields. Following the yellow marker arrows cross the first two fields with the hedge on your left. Continue straight across the next field keeping to the left of a line of trees and then cross three more fields with a hedge on your right. At the end of the final field cross a stile and continue forward to the brow of the hill, from where there is a dramatic view of Creswell Colliery. It is difficult to reconcile this bleak, industrial landscape with the quiet, rural view in the opposite direction.

Continue forward down the hill to find a clear path which bears right down the hillside and leads eventually to a stile at the start of the limestone gorge. Cross the small bridge over the river and turn right along a path which runs the length of the gorge. The famous Creswell caves can be seen in the cliffs on either side. The path continues past the small man-made lake and on back to the Visitors' Centre.

Note: The Visitors' Centre opens on Sundays throughout the year and other opening varies according to the time of year. Up-to-date information on opening can be obtained by contacting the Peacock Information and Heritage Centre, Chesterfield.

THE PIN HOLE CAVE, CRESWELL CRAGS

Cutthorpe - Old Brampton - Pratthall - Newgate - Cutthorpe

A walk through fields and woodlands, on the western boundary of Chesterfield, which skirts the 19th century Linacre reservoirs and passes through several pleasant villages.

Distance: Just over 5 miles (8 km).
Parking: On the roadside opposite the Methodist Chapel at Cutthorpe. Map reference 347735.
Time: Allowing time to visit Old Brampton church, just over 3 hours.

ON the opposite side of the road to the Methodist Chapel a stile beside a gate leads into the fields. The path is straight ahead over two fields and just before some farm buildings it turns right over a stile. Follow the wall on the left and go through another stile into the lane leading to Cutthorpe Hall.

Turn left and a little way beyond the Hall gates look for a well-trodden path on the right leading into the trees. Walk through the trees to where the path opens out into a field and go straight ahead to the next field. Continue forward with a hedge on the right, climb another stile and then bear left diagonally across the field following a well-worn path to a stile leading into a wood. A few paces into the wood turn left to join another path and almost immediately find a stile on the right which leads through the trees and into a field. The path over this field is not clear but bear left diagonally across the field to find a wooden stile a little to the left of a small concrete building.

The path crosses a footbridge, then a wide track and continues straight ahead up the opposite slope. Where the slope levels out keep to the obvious path just inside the wood with a wall on the left. Continue to where a path from the lowest reservoir joins from the right and here turn left over a stile into a field. There is a clear path across this field making for a stile on the left in the opposite corner. From here climb the fields to reach Old Brampton churchyard. This ancient parish church has some interesting features and is well worth a visit. Can you spot the mistake made in the painting of the clock face?

Turn right along the road beyond the church and continue for about ¼ of a mile. Where the road bends left shortly after passing a second wooden seat a signposted footpath leads off to the right immediately before a house. Keeping to the wall on the right, pass a farm and a

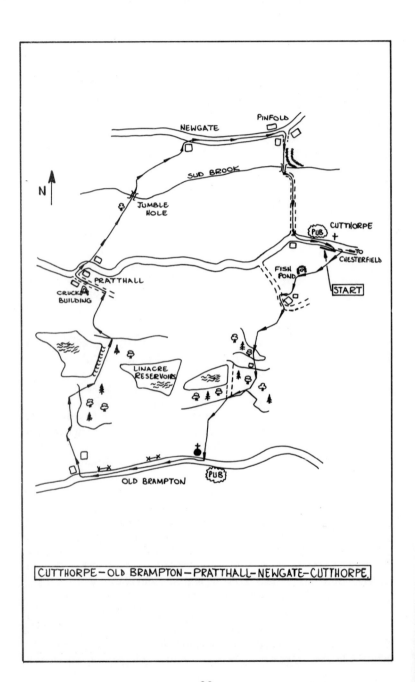

NEWGATE

PINFOLD

SUD BROOK

N

JUMBLE HOLE

CUTTHORPE

PUB

TO CHESTERFIELD

FISH POND

START

PRATTHALL

CRUCK BUILDING

LINACRE RESERVOIRS

OLD BRAMPTON

PUB

CUTTHORPE–OLD BRAMPTON–PRATTHALL–NEWGATE–CUTTHORPE.

short distance into the third field climb a stile on the right. Bearing left cross the field diagonally and aim to the left of the woods. Take the stile in the wall ahead and keeping the wall on the right cross one field and when partly across the second find a stile on the right which soon leads through a plantation and to the embankment of the highest of the Linacre Reservoirs. The views from the embankment are superb in both directions. There are three reservoirs in this complex built to provide water for the local area; the top and bottom ones being built around 1855 and the middle one being added in 1904.

Cross the embankment and continue forward over a stone stile into the wood and uphill to find a wooden stile leading into the field above. Hereabouts, in season, can be seen cowslips, violets, wood anemones and a profusion of bluebells. Bear left across the field following the obvious path to a squeezer stile on the right which leads up across two fields and over a step stile into the lane at the hamlet of Pratthall. Turn left along this lane passing a long, low building on the left. This is the original 'hall', an ancient cruck building, which until the 1960s was used in the traditional way of housing the family at one end of the building and animals in the rest. At a later date the building now known as Pratt Hall was constructed on the opposite side of the lane.

Turn right on reaching the road and continue until a stone stile on the left is reached immediately before the first house. Go through the stile and keeping near the hedge on the right cross two fields and after passing through a stone stile go straight forward across the third field to pass a solitary tree and find, amongst trees, a stone footbridge over the Sud Brook. This secluded spot is called Jumble Hole which in the past denoted a 'rough, low-lying, bushy, uncultivated hollow'. Of the many places in England bearing this name there can be few which match the description more aptly.

Cross the bridge and walk up a steep well-worn path and over a stile into a field. Go straight forward towards a small barn but just before reaching it turn right and keeping the hedge on the left continue to find another wooden stile into the next field. From here aim towards Newgate Farm finding stiles on the left of the first gate and the right of the second. On approaching the farm keep to the left of the buildings and make for a stone stile in the wall on the right under trees above the farm. The path goes through the copse and emerges onto the road at Newgate. As you continue in the same direction along the road there are fine views over Chesterfield to Bolsover Castle and Hardwick Hall before you reach the old Barlow Pinfold on the left. This 200-year-old stone enclosure was used in times past to hold stray animals until claimed by their owners. It has been unused for over a hundred years but was listed as a protected building in 1967 and has recently been restored. The name 'Barlow' was chiselled from the stone above the doorway as part of the local plan to make difficulties for invaders during the last war.

Just past the pinfold where the road bends left a track leads off to the right between two houses. A little way down the track ignore a stile on the left, take a stile leading into the field ahead and continue, keeping the hedge on the left. At the bottom of the field, where the hedge bears left, go straight ahead to cross a small footbridge over the Sud Brook. More adventurous types - with wellies - might prefer to ignore the previous stile and follow the overgrown 'holloway', which starts beside the stile, down to the stream. Over the footbridge follow the obvious path which leads uphill, bearing left, and into the surfaced Common Lane, taking you back to the main road at Cutthorpe.

On reaching the main road the building opposite is the former Cutthorpe School built 1865 but superseded by the existing school building in 1884. Since then it has been used for church services, as a library and as a reading room where villagers who wanted to improve thier knowledge would gather to hear the local newspapers read to them. The tree with the seat around was planted by the villagers in 1911 to commemorate the coronation of George V.

Turn left and walk down the road to the starting point.

Eckington - Plumbley - Ridgeway - Eckington

A walk on the borders of North Derbyshire and South Yorkshire which passes through the quiet, wooded Moss valley and onto the surrounding hills from which there are outstanding views.

Distance: Just over 6 miles (10 km).
Parking: On the roadside near Eckington church.
Time: Almost 4 hours.

WALK a little way along Mill Road and turn right down a footpath alongside the churchyard wall. Passing the fine Norman west doorway of the church follow the path across a footbridge and turn left at the end of the trees. Keep to the field edge until you reach the road. Turn left down the road for a few yards and then right onto a wide track leading into the trees above the Moss Brook. This quiet, wooded valley has not always had a peaceful, rural aspect. The waters of the Moss and adjoining streams were once used to drive wheels for grinding the scythes and sickles for which the area was noted and the remains of several dams can be seen along the way.

Continue along this obvious track for some distance, ignoring turnings to the left and right, until just before the track bears left to a wooden footbridge, a gateway marked 'Private - No road' appears ahead. Just before the gateway cross a stile on the right and immediately turn left to follow the path up the fieldside with the hedge and woods on your left. The view back towards Eckington from here is superb. Soon the path goes slightly downhill and re-enters the trees bringing you quickly to the junction of several paths. Turn right up a wide grassed track. This sunken track was the line of a tramway - known locally as a 'drag-road' - by means of which coal was hauled from the Footrail colliery in the valley bottom to a weighbridge at Plumbley. It has been disused since the middle of the 19th century.

A little way up the trackway look for paths leading off to the right and left. Follow the path on the left straight across the corner of a field and then along the edge of the field with the trees on your left. Towards the end of the field the path turns slightly left and crosses a stile through bushes and into the next field. A short distance into this field bear right and keeping near the gorse bushes on the right climb the field to where the ground levels and a stile in a fence appears ahead.

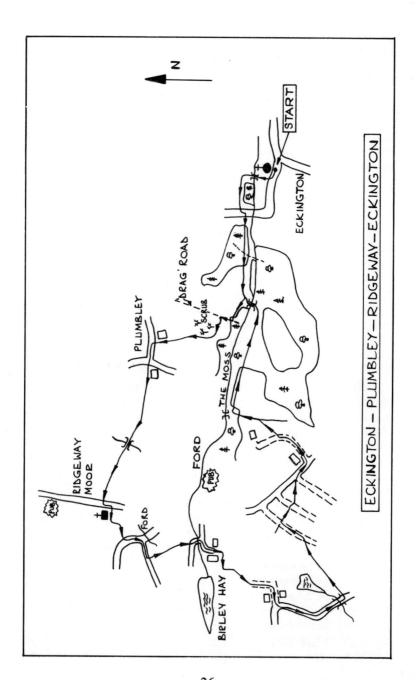

ECKINGTON – PLUMBLEY – RIDGEWAY – ECKINGTON

26

Cross the stile and make towards the left of a house and over a stile into Plumbley Lane. Turn left and on reaching the junction with another lane go through the stile beside the gate opposite.

Continue forward through two stiles and into a large field. The path climbs steadily across the field to a stile on the brow of the hill from where there are magnificent views in several directions. Cross the stile and bear right to follow the obvious path around the field edge to the far righthand corner. Ignore the stile on the left and continue forward between a fence and a low wall to reach a stile on the right. From here the path is clear down to a footbridge over a stream. Bearing right at the other side of the stream ignore a stile in the hedge on the right part way up the field and climb to a stile at the top right-hand corner. Continue along the obvious path around the next field keeping the hedge on your right. Where the hedge ends by a solitary tree turn right and walk with another hedge on the left along the field side and down a pleasant tree-lined track to reach the road at Ridgeway Moor.

Turn left down the road to a lane on the right immediately below the church. Follow the lane until a gate just beyond a left-hand bend is reached. Take the path to the left of the gate between high hedges which takes you down steps and into another lane. Turn left and just before the ford bear right following the surfaced lane uphill to a farm. A little way beyond the farm buildings go through a stile on the left and cross two fields, keeping the hedge on your left in both, to reach the lane at Birleyhay. This secluded hamlet was the site of an old established sickle works whose 'cutler whele' was first referred to in 1599. The works had a large export trade in the early 1800s. Go straight forward over a bridge and immediately turn right into a lane.

Follow this lane between stone gateposts and beyond the modernised farmhouse turn right to cross a stile. From the next section of the route you can see the lowest of the three dams which powered the grinding wheels at Birleyhay and which is now a favourite haunt of herons and other water birds. Keeping the field boundary on the right cross another stile and then turn left over the next stile at the end of the field. Follow the hedge on the right for a short distance then turn right over a stile and bear left, crossing the field diagonally to reach a stile leading into a green lane. At the end of the green lane climb the stile to turn right into a track which leads into the road beyond Fold Farm.

Turn left to walk along the road for some distance and shortly after crossing a small bridge look for a stile and a footpath sign beside a gateway on the left. The path is very narrow and overgrown here between a low wall and a wire fence but a stile into the field on the right is soon reached. Bear left and cross the field diagonally to a stile on the left of a wooden fence, then continue in the same direction across the next two fields crossing two more wooden stiles before reaching a prominent electricity pylon on the hillside. Following the line of the pylons brings you via a stile to the right of a gate into a bridleway.

Turn left along this track and when a house appears ahead start looking for a clear wooden stile on the right just beyond the point where another path comes in on the left. Cross the stile and bear left to find a stile in the hedge a short way up the field. Over the stile follow the hedge on the right to cross a farm track and climb another stile almost immediately opposite. Now bear left over the hill passing between two large gorse patches to find a stile in the left-hand corner of the field. Cross the main road and walk a few yards to the right to where a turning to Habberjam Farm is indicated. Go down this lane, passing the house on the left, and continue for some distance to where the lane bears left on reaching a field. Turn right and walk across the top edge of the field and on meeting a footpath down the opposite side turn left and follow the well-worn path down the fields to the stream in the wood below.

Turn right just before the footbridge and follow a clear path across the bottom of a field and then into the wood. In spring the display of marsh marigolds along here is rivalled only by the abundance of bluebells seen throughout the walk. Continue along the wide track above the stream until you reach a point where several paths converge. Here turn left, cross the footbridge and take the clear track bearing right and uphill. From here return to Eckington along the same path on which you started off.

Hardwick Hall - Ault Hucknall - Hardwick Hall

A walk in the neighbourhood of Hardwick Hall which is short enough to allow time for a visit to this well-known Derbyshire mansion.

Distance: About 3 miles (5 km).
Parking: The car park at Hardwick Hall.
Time: About 1½ hours.

FROM the car park turn right into the road and follow it for some distance. The road can be quite busy at times as it is the main route to the hall but a very wide grass verge beside it makes walking pleasant. Shortly after a gate-house the road forks. Here turn left and after a short distance you will find a stile in the hedge on the left. Climb the stile and bear slightly right across the fields making towards Ault Hucknall ahead. The path regains the road shortly before the hamlet. Follow the road through Ault Hucknall passing the church on the right. The church is small but interesting and well worth a visit. It contains remnants of stonework from the Saxon church which occupied the site over a thousand years ago and a uniquely carved Norman arch portraying several biblical themes including the Creation and the Flood. The church also contains the tomb of Thomas Hobbes the great 17th century philosopher who had connections with Hardwick Hall. An attractive modern feature is the collection of colourful and decorative hassocks depicting local scenes and industries.

Just past the church turn left along a rough driveway across the fields. Where the driveway swings right immediately beyond a house continue straight ahead through a gate into Hardwick Park. Follow the fence on your right and where it turns sharply to the right continue forward. Bear slightly right and go downhill aiming between two fenced-in clumps of young trees. After passing a triangular wooden seat on your right the path dips and crosses a grassy track just before reaching a gate in the fence. Through the gate continue in the same direction making for the trees to the right of the Great Pond visible ahead. On reaching the fence find a small gate to the right of a larger one bringing you onto a clear track. Climb the stile on the left and walk up the track beside the small ponds. Follow the obvious track leading between two ponds and cross the stile at the far side. Now bear slightly

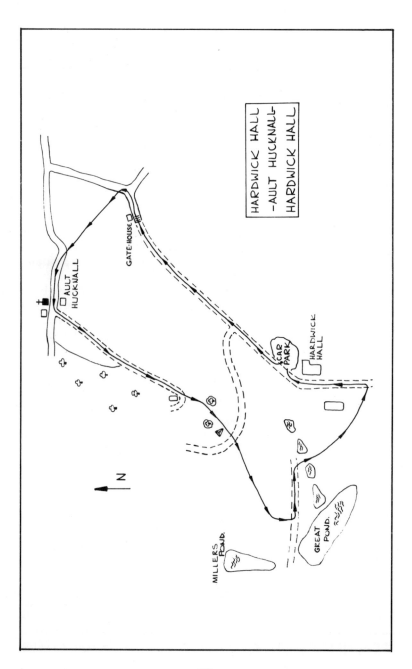

HARDWICK HALL
-AULT HUCKNALL-
HARDWICK HALL

GATE-HOUSE

AULT
HUCKNALL

HARDWICK
HALL

CAR
PARK

N

MILLERS
POND.

GREAT
POND.

left and aim up the hill towards the ruins of the old Hall at the top. The trackway gradually becomes clearer and leads to the road just below Hardwick Hall. Turn left into the road which leads past the Hall and back to the car park.

Hardwick Hall is an impressive Tudor mansion built by Bess of Hardwick who acquired great wealth and social importance through four judicious marriages. It was built between 1591 and 1597, was the last of her building ventures and was exceptional in its large number of windows. A local saying goes 'Hardwick Hall - more glass than wall'. The ruins opposite are the remains of the old Hall which Bess had barely finished constructing when she started work on her new house.

Note: While Hardwick Park is open all year round the House and Gardens are usually open only from Easter to the end of October. Up-to-date information on opening can be obtained by contacting the Peacock Information and Heritage Centre, Chesterfield.

MILLTHORPE — CARTLEDGE — BARLOW WOODSEATS — MILLTHORPE.

CARTLEDGE HALL
CARTLEDGE

N

WATERCRESS BED

CAR PARKING

PUB

MILLTHORPE

MILLTHORPE BROOK

DUNSTON BROOK

BARLOW WOODSEATS
CRUCK BARN

HARKER WOOD

CRUCK BARN

RUMBLING STREET

Millthorpe - Cartledge - Barlow Woodseats - Millthorpe

A pleasant walk along tracks and through fields giving splendid views from both sides of the Cordwell Valley and passing several interesting old buildings.

Distance: Just under 4 miles (6 km).
Parking: At the bottom of Millthorpe Lane. Map reference 317764.
Time: About 2½ hours.

WALK up Millthorpe Lane to turn left along the bridleway signposted to Horsleygate Lane. Almost immediately cross the wooden stile on the right and follow the path uphill over the fields keeping near the hedge on the left. Part way across the third field a gravelled path leads left to a small wooden footbridge over a stream. Now bear right and continue uphill with the hedge on the right. After passing an impressive watercres bed on the right climb three stiles to eventually reach a footpath sign beside another stile on the right. Cross the stile and bear slightly left uphill to reach a track leading onto the road at Cartledge.

Turn left into the road and then turn right past Cartledge Hall. This interesting old house was built in 1492 by the owner of nearby Horsleygate. Little is known of its history, though it was probably a farmhouse for much of the time. By 1947 it was semi-derelict and was saved from demolition when a local man bought it and restored it to its present fine condition. The quiet hamlet of Cartledge provides a perfect setting for this attractive example of early craftsmanship. Continue past the Equestrian Centre and straight ahead down a rough lane for some distance to reach a slight right-hand bend with gates on both sides and a cross-country jump beside the one on the left. Turn left through the gate and continue downhill keeping the hedge close on your right. At the bottom of the field climb a step stile over a wall and continue forward along a path, which becomes more distinct, until a gate and a stile in the hedge on the right are reached shortly before the end of the field.

Cross the bridleway and go through the gate opposite to follow the path downhill bearing sharp left through the second gateway and soon climb a stile into a lane. Turn right and a few steps along look for a footpath sign among the trees on the left. Follow the path over a stile

THE BRIDGE OVER DUNSTON BROOK

Alison Russell

and continue forward keeping the hedge on the left to cross a bridge over the Dunston Brook and reach the road.

Almost opposite is a footpath signposted 'Rumbling Street'. The path follows the hedge on the left through four fields to the corner of Harker Wood. At this point it is worth pausing to admire the view back across to Cartledge and to investigate what appears to be an unusual form of stile. In fact it is an arrangement in the field boundary wall which makes it possible for riders with the local hunt to jump the wall at whatever height is suitable for their horse. Continue forward with the trees on your right until turning left uphill at the next fence and over a stile made with disused millstones into Far Lane.

Turn right and walk up the road past Rumbling Street Farm, the barn of which is described in the other Millthorpe walk. At the far end of a small wood on the right is a trackway to Barlow Woodseats. Follow the track through the farm and where the driveway turns right around the end of another impressive cruck barn go through the gate on the left. Interesting features of this 14th century barn are its obvious ventilation holes and windows at one end of a design which suggests it might at some time have been used as a chapel. In its considerable length it still retains five sets of supporting cruck timbers.

The path goes slightly left, downhill and over a stile into a track which is often very muddy. Continue through the stile opposite, over a small brook and then bear slightly right across the field towards a gateway and stile beside a tall tree. Keep to the hedge on the right down the next field to climb a stile at the bottom and turn left over a footbridge. Go diagonally across the next field to a stile in the right-hand corner then follow the hedge to emerge through a gateway into a lane. Turn left and follow the lane over the brook and back to the starting point.

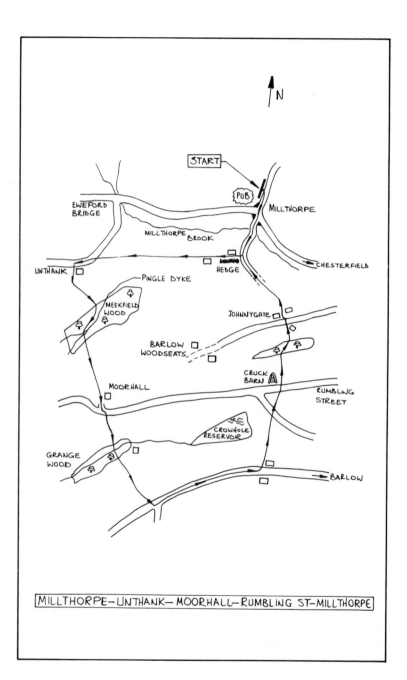

MILLTHORPE—UNTHANK—MOORHALL—RUMBLING ST—MILLTHORPE

Millthorpe - Unthank - Moorhall - Rumbling Street - Millthorpe

A route through undulating countryside along well-established field footpaths which go through a small wood, around a reservoir and past an ancient 'cruck' barn.

Distance: Approximately 4 miles (6.5 km).
Parking: At the bottom of Millthorpe Lane. Map reference 317764.
Time: About 2½ hours.

FROM the bottom of Millthorpe Lane cross the road and go down Mill Lane and over the ford. A few paces further up the lane turn right along a narrow path which runs between a fence and a hedge. Don't be put off by the over-grown start as the path soon improves. The path passes close to a house after a short distance then into fields from which there is a pleasant view down over Millthorpe Brook. Keeping the hedge on the left cross the fields and stiles to emerge into a lane on a bend at Unthank. Go forward up the lane to find a stile beside a gate beyond the second house on the left. Pass through this stile, cross the field and go through the stile by the gateway almost straight ahead. Do note the great width of the hedges in this area which probably means that they are very old boundary markers. Follow the path keeping to the hedge on your left and cross the stile into Meekfield Wood. In autumn a wide variety of fungi can be found here.

Turn right and follow the clear path which goes slightly uphill at first and then drops down to the left across a stream and continues steeply up to emerge into the field below Moorhall Farm. Keep the line of bushes and the stream on your right and when they end continue up the field to reach a step stile to the right of the farm buildings. At the end of the building cross the stile over the wall on the left into a track which leads to the road beyond.

Turn left along the road and at the next left-hand bend go over the stile on the right at the start of a farm track. Go uphill to the white gate on the right and then bear right and follow the wall downhill to the stile. Walk straight ahead over the next field to the stone stile in the wall and cross another field to reach a stile through the wall into Grange Wood. The path is clear, down over a footbridge and up the other side into the field above Grange Lumb Farm.

Go over a stone step stile which is straight ahead beyond the farm track. The next stile is not very evident being partly obscured by the surrounding holly hedge but once found it is easily negotiated. Once over bear slightly right uphill to a step stile in the wall half way up the next field. Now follow the wall. Beyond this field there is a well-defined track which reaches the road below Barlow Grange.

Turn left and follow the road for about half a mile to High Ashes Farm. The footpath to take is indicated at the side of a barn on the left of the road and is easily followed downhill towards Crowhole Reservoir. When approaching the trees to the right of the reservoir aim for the right-hand corner of the field and the path goes down the side of the trees and turns sharp right to a gate which leads onto the road.

On the opposite side of the road and a few yards to the right take the footpath over the stile, turn left and go over a plank bridge. Keeping the thick hedge on your right climb the fields to Rumbling Street. The name 'Rumbling Street' is said to indicate a lesser known Roman road, part of the network of roads over which in Roman times pigs of lead were brought to Chesterfield. Before continuing the walk do stop and investigate the cruck barn, now used as a garage, which stands end-on to the road. The barn is often left conveniently open which allows a chance to admire the impressive cruck timbers. This type of building, with its massive wooden framework, is thought to have been introduced by the North European people who settled in the area after the Romans had departed. They were skilled boat builders and used their knowledge of trees and timber to build a strong homestead on their chosen site.

The path now goes through the gate to the right of the farm buildings and over a stile to the left of the stables. Follow the track downhill and to the right, then go straight on towards a small wood. Keep to the right of the trees at first and then go over a stile into the wood. The path is clear from here to Johnnygate, emerging into the road over a stile by the gate to the left of the barn in the last field.

Almost opposite take the track between the farmhouse and the farm buildings and go through the gate to follow the hedge on the left down the fields, cross a footbridge and eventually go over a stile and into the lane. The ford and the starting point are a few minutes walk up the lane.

Old Whittington - Hundall - Old Whittington

A walk around a surprisingly quiet and attractive upland area above industrialised valleys.

Distance: Just over 4 miles (7 km).
Parking: In the public car park opposite Revolution House,
*   Old Whittington. Map reference 385749.*
Time: About 2¼ hours, but allow time to visit the museum.

THIS walk starts and finishes at Revolution House. In 1688 this building was known as the Cock and Pynot Inn - pynot being a local name for the magpie - and it was here that the fourth Earl of Devonshire and two other leading opponents of James II met to plot his dethronement and the accession of William of Orange. Today the charming cottage houses a small museum dedicated to commemorating the event. At one time Old Whittington had a thriving glass-making industry and a collection of what are thought to be the only surviving objects of 'Whittington Glass' are also on display there.

Walk along Church Street North to the left of Revolution House for about ½ a mile. A little way beyond a pub called The Poplar find a stile in the wall on the right just before the road forks. The path leads between houses and into a field. Follow the clear path over stiles and a footbridge until reaching a stile in a wire fence at the far side of the fourth field. Go through the stile and with the stream close on your left the path soon leads to a footbridge over the stream.

Cross the bridge and continue along a well-worn path keeping to a wall and hedge on the right. On reaching the end of a small wood keep straight ahead up the field, passing to the left of two trees and reaching a stile which climbs the wall into the next field. From here the path is usually clear but if it is not bear slightly left and make for the middle of the line of trees ahead, keeping to the right of some bushes just before the wood. Follow the wide track straight ahead through the wood, over a ladder stile, across another track and onto the field beyond the wood. Continue forward keeping to the wire fence on the right. At the far side of the field ignore the stile on the right and make for the stile ahead which leads into a track.

A short way along the track take the right-hand fork and go on through old industrial workings. On reaching the lane below cross

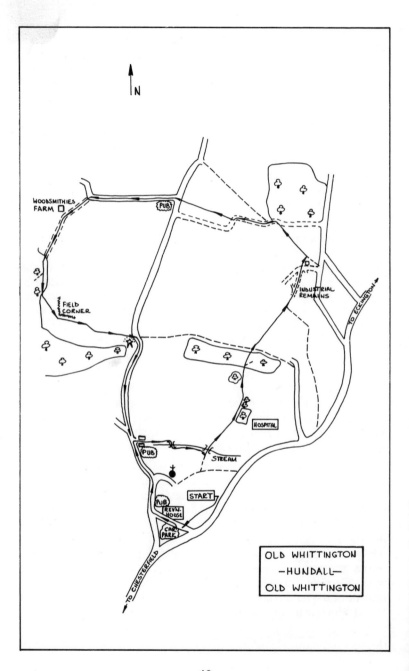

N

WOODSMITHIES FARM

PUB

FIELD CORNER

INDUSTRIAL REMAINS

TO ECKINGTON

HOSPITAL

PUB

STREAM

PUB
REVN. HOUSE

START

CAR PARK

TO CHESTERFIELD

OLD WHITTINGTON
—HUNDALL—
OLD WHITTINGTON

over, go through a stile and keeping to the left of the house go through another stile and into a field beyond. Bearing right go diagonally over the field until another path is met at right-angles part way across the field. Turn left along this path to find a wooden stile at the field corner bringing you into a rough lane. Turn left and continue along the lane, which becomes narrower and unsurfaced, until just after it bends sharply to the left you find a stile on the right. Go over the stile and walk straight forward across two fields to continue along a narrow path between a hedge and a fence and emerge into the road at Hundall.

Cross the road and continue in the same direction passing the Miners' Arms on the left. This building was formerly Gaitlands Farm until it became a public house in 1858 and the name 'Miners' Arms' is a reference to the many small coal mines which were worked in the Hundall area. Where the road bends sharply to the right turn down a rough lane on the left and after a short distance pass Woodsmithies Farm on your right. Woodsmithies was one of the principal homesteads in the parish of Unstone, being first recorded in 1329, and its name indicates the activity that was carried on at the site centuries ago. The fields around are rich in iron-bearing stone and traces of coal-mining by the early bell-pit and later drift mine methods have been found in the adjoining Ramshaw Woods. Continue into the wood, and ignoring turnings to the right climb the track through the trees to reach the field ahead. The path across the field is not clear but it bears left to climb the field diagonally and reach the hedged corner of an adjoining field. Continue forward keeping to the hedge on the left until almost at the end of the field and then bear right to the gateway ahead. The path is clear now, with a hedge on the left, until the road just above the T.V. mast is reached. Turn right into the road.

This road gives magnificent views over Chesterfield and a wide expanse of North East Derbyshire and takes you back to Old Whittington.

Note: Revolution House is usually open from Wednesday to Saturday inclusive during the period May Day to mid-September. Up-to-date information on opening can be obtained by contacting the Peacock Information and Heritage Centre, Chesterfield.

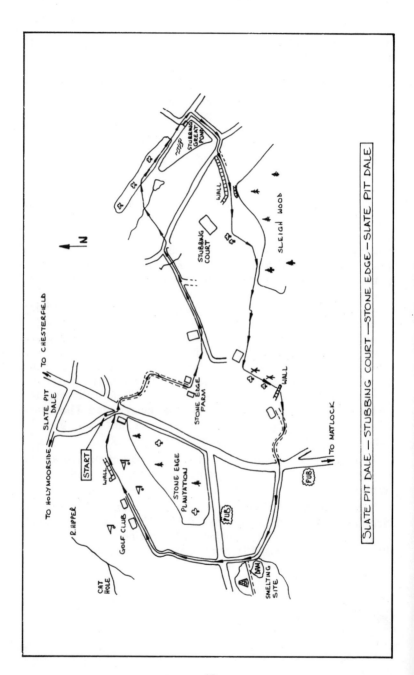

SLATE PIT DALE — STUBBING COURT — STONE EDGE — SLATE PIT DALE

Slate Pit Dale - Stubbing Court - Stone Edge - Slate Pit Dale

Field footpaths, farm tracks and short stretches of quiet road lead around Stubbing Great Pond, through quiet countryside and on to an important 18th century industrial site.

Distance: Almost 5 miles (7.5 km).
Parking: About 4 miles out of Chesterfield on the A 632 Matlock road turn right down a side road which comes immediately before Stone Edge Plantation and is signposted 'Holymoorside'. Park on the roadside. Map reference 345677.
Time: Allowing time to explore the industrial site, the walk will take about 3 hours.

WALK back to the main Chesterfield road, cross it and find a footpath sign on the left at the start of a farm track. Before descending the track stop and admire the extensive view from this point. Follow the track until it reaches Stone Edge Farm and in the farmyard find a step stile over the wall on the left immediately after a large barn. Go over the stile and walk down the field keeping to the wall on the left until you come to another stile beside a gate. Cross the stile and go straight forward to reach the poultry farm driveway. Turn left and follow the drive downhill and across a ford until it joins a minor road. Continue along the road in the same direction to reach a footpath on the left signposted to Swathwick.

Climb the step stile in the wall and bearing slightly right cross the field to find a footbridge over a small stream. Bear right and follow the clear path up to a stile which leads into a wood. Continue on the path along the top of the wood. In autumn when the many chestnut trees shed their fruit squirrels are much in evidence foraging among the leaves and leaping through the branches. At the end of the wood continue straight ahead across a field and emerge into a narrow road. Turn right and right again along a road signposted 'Ashover' which crosses the lower end of Stubbing Great Pond. Although its name now connects it with nearby Stubbing Court this lake was constructed by the owners of the now demolished Wingerworth Hall.

On meeting the road at the other side of the lake turn right and almost immediately left up a track signposted 'Stone Edge'. Follow the track keeping to the wall on the right until shortly after the third stile the track becomes walled on both sides and opens out into a field. At this point bear right diagonally across the field to a stile and gateway near two large trees. From here can be seen Stubbing Court, an imposing residence most of which was built in the middle of the 18th century. In the 1830s it was the home of the Right Honourable James Abercrombie, a well-known local dignitary, and towards the end of the 19th century the future Lady Baden-Powell was born here.

Having turned your back on Stubbing Court cross the stile and keeping the hedge and fence on your left walk on to the next stile which leads into a field immediately before a pine wood. Turn right through the stile and almost immediately cross into the next field. Bear left to reach the wall of Sleigh Wood and then continue with the wood on your left to a stile and a gateway beside the end of the wood. Now make for the footpath sign which can be seen straight ahead across the next field. Here climb the stile over the wall and then continue in the same direction as before keeping the hedge close on the right. On reaching a large holly tree immediately beyond the first house on the right, turn left up the hill following the direction of the overhead power lines. At the wall in front on a level with the farm climb a somewhat derelict stile then bearing slightly right find a stile in the wall opposite leading into a lane just above the main farm buildings. Continue up the lane to the main road.

Take the minor road directly opposite and walk on until Stone Edge smelting site, with its prominent chimney, is reached. This was one of many such lead smelts on the moorlands around this part of Derbyshire and was probably developed during the 18th century. The complicated system of flues to condense the poisonous fumes is still evident on the ground as is the small dam which is thought to have been used to power a water wheel. The recently repaired chimney is said to be the oldest existing industrial chimney in Britain. The site is well worth exploring.

Continue along the road and on coming to the minor cross-roads follow the road opposite leading to Stanedge Golf Club. The view from this road down over Cat Hole and the valley of the Hipper is magnificent. On reaching a farm beyond the club house climb over the stile and continue straight ahead to reach a wall on the left. Keeping as near to the wall as the gorse bushes allow follow the path until the main Chesterfield road comes into view. Bear right across the final field to reach a gate on the left of two houses and you are back at the starting point.

STONE EDGE CHIMNEY.

J. Russell.

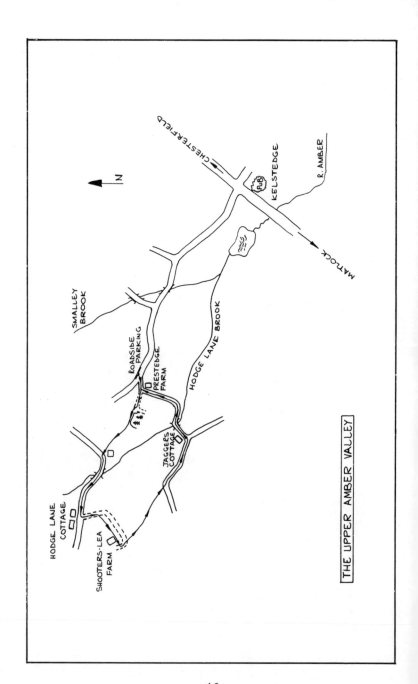

THE UPPER AMBER VALLEY

The Upper Amber Valley

A short walk in a peaceful and little-known valley whose fast-flowing brooks combine to become the river Amber.

Distance: 1½ miles (2½ km).

Parking: Turn off the main Chesterfield - Matlock road almost opposite the inn at Kelstedge. Follow the lane towards Uppertown and park on the roadside near Prestedge Farm. Map reference 326645.

Time: About an hour.

TAKE the left-hand fork of the road making towards a wind-pump visible ahead. Where the road turns sharply left at Prestedge Farm go forward along a farm track. When this track also bends left cross into the field on the right and continue in the same direction alongside a spruce plantation on your left. At the end of the plantation continue forward across the corner of the field to meet the hedge on the left. Keeping to the hedge go through a squeezer stile into the next field and continue forward to eventually climb a step stile into the lane just above a farm.

Turn left and follow the road down to the Hodge Lane Brook. This is one of the small, unassuming streams which soon combine to form the river Amber. It is easy to see from the speed of this contributary how useful the river was in powering the many mills along its 12 mile course a century or so ago. Continue up the road passing Hodge Lane Cottage on your right to take a rough track on the left which leads to Shooters-Lea Farm. Walk up the track and shortly after a stile over the fence go up the bank on the right and through a stile in the wall. Go straight up the field and when the farm comes into view make for a gate just to the left of the buildings. Through the gate continue forward and through another small gate to re-join the farm track.

Turn left and climb a rather derelict stile beside the gate opposite. Follow the obvious track over the fields to eventually reach a road. Turn left and walk down the road to keep left again at a road junction. The house beside the road here is called Jaggers Cottage. A jagger was the man in charge of a string of pack-horses - the most common means of transporting goods across this part of the country as late as the mid-19th century. The lane that the cottage stands by is part of the old pack-horse route linking the bridge over the Derwent at Darley Dale with the Amber valley.

Follow the road back to the car.